I can do all things through him who strengthens me.
—*Philippians* 4:13

WHAT WOULD JESUS DO?

Randy Petersen

new seasons
™

a division of Publications International, Ltd.

Randy Petersen studied ancient languages at Wheaton College before becoming executive editor of Bible Newsletter and other publications. Currently a full-time freelance writer and editor, he has contributed to more than 20 books. He is coauthor of *Jesus: His Life and Times*.

ISBN: 0-7853-3849-7

WHAT WOULD JESUS DO...

...when you're worried about your loved ones?

So do not worry about tomorrow, for tomorrow will bring worries of its own. Today's trouble is enough for today.

—*Matthew* 6:34

IT'S ONE THING TO WORRY ABOUT yourself, about your own health, wealth, and comfort. But worrying about others is another matter. This kind of worry starts with love. You care about these people, and so you want what's best for them and you worry that things might go wrong for them. What could be wrong with that?

Well, worry is destructive. It gnaws at your nerves. It robs you of joy.

Worrying about others is especially difficult because you have less control. Scientific experiments have shown that rats go crazy when they have no control over their situation. People aren't much different. Ultimately, you have little control over the lives of the loved ones you worry about. What can you do besides worry?

Do not worry about anything, but in everything by prayer and supplication with thanksgiving let your requests be made known to God.
—*Philippians 4:6*

You COULD TRY PRAYING. THAT'S what Jesus did when he was concerned about Simon Peter. "Satan has demanded to sift all of you like wheat," Jesus said. "But I have prayed for you that your own faith may not fail" (Luke 22:31-32).

Worry is the opposite of faith. If you really believe that the Lord cares about your loved ones, you can trust him to manage things. So throw your worries away. Toss them to the Lord.

Jesus began to weep.

—John 11:35

JESUS WAS NOT AFRAID TO SHOW HIS emotions. He laughed and cried and teased and complained and sometimes had to get away by himself. Was he ever depressed? Probably. He cried over the city of Jerusalem as it rejected him. He often commented on the "little faith" of his disciples. After three years of traveling with him, they still weren't getting it. Despite his divinity, the very human Jesus had to have down times.

But he didn't get stuck there. He moved on. He stepped steadily forward

on his mission.

That's the key to beating depression: Keep moving. Most of us have a natural cycle of emotions. We get depressed for a while—usually after something has gone wrong for us—and then we recover. As surely as water falls to earth, evaporates to the skies, and falls again, this cycle will continue.

For everything there is a season, and a time for every matter under heaven: . . . a time to weep, and a time to laugh; a time to mourn, and a time to dance.

—*Ecclesiastes 3:1,4*

*S*OMETIMES PEOPLE GET THE IDEA THAT it's not "righteous" to be sad. Christians ought to rejoice all the time, right? As a result, people hide their depression . . . and stay in it longer. No, it's better to be honest about your feelings—with God, with yourself, with everyone else. Even in your bad mood, you can appreciate the fact that the Lord is with you.

When my way is drear, precious Lord, linger
  near.
When the day is almost gone,
Hear my cry, hear my call,
Hold my hand, lest I fall,
Precious Lord, take my hand, lead me home.
—*Traditional Spiritual*

WHAT WOULD JESUS DO . . .

*. . . when you've done
something very wrong?*

∞

TWO DISCIPLES: JUDAS AND PETER.
Both hurt Jesus and felt terrible about
what they had done. It was Judas, of
course, who engineered Jesus' arrest,
leading the soldiers to Jesus' hideout,
betraying him with a kiss. Later, in
remorse, he returned his bribe money,
saying, "I have sinned by betraying
innocent blood" (Matthew 27:4). Then
he went out and hanged himself. He
just couldn't see any way back into
God's good graces.

Peter's story started out similarly.
Three times he denied knowing Jesus,

saving his own skin rather than standing up for his Master. Afterward, he "wept bitterly." But in John 21 we read a fascinating conversation between Peter and the risen Jesus. Three times Jesus asks if Peter loves him. And three times—once for each of his earlier denials—Peter says yes.

Turn the page to Acts chapter 1 and it's the forgiven Peter who announces Judas' suicide to the apostles. Peter went on to become a dynamic leader of the Church. Forgiveness made all the difference.

If we confess our sins, he who is faithful and just will forgive us our sins and cleanse us from all unrighteousness.

—1 John 1:9

Lord, I messed up.
Big time.
I guess I'm not the Chris-
    tian I thought I was.
I hurt you, I know.
I hurt myself, I hurt
    others, I know, I know,
    I know.

And I'm sorry, I'm sorry, I'm sorry, I'm sorry,
    I'm sorry, I'm sorry, I'm sorry.
I wish I could go back in time,
Undoing all of it.
Can I ever make up for what I did?
Can you ever forgive me?
Please?

I am a sinner.
You are a Savior.
Bring me back to your love.

*There is therefore now no condemnation for those
    who are in Christ Jesus.*

—*Romans* 8:1

WHAT WOULD JESUS DO...

...when you're grieving?

He was... a man of sorrows, and familiar with suffering.

—Isaiah 53:3 *(NIV)*

WHEN YOU'RE GRIEVING—WHETHER it's the death of a loved one or some other life crisis—your biggest problems often come from well-meaning people. They try to cheer you up, as if it's wrong to feel sad. Jesus had times of laughter, too, but what a comfort it is to know that this prophecy also describes him. He can sympathize with us because he was "familiar with suffering."

Lord, this one who shared my life
Has left this earth to share your life
In a far better world.
I miss this one I grew to love,
I miss the smile, the life, the love
This dear one had
   to share.
Sometimes I get
   mad at you
For taking this one
   home to you
And leaving me
   alone.
But I know you will
   bolster me
With hugs from
   those who comfort me,
With healing words and sympathy.
I'll bask in happy memories
And make my life a eulogy
Until in your eternity
We share our life again.

WHAT WOULD JESUS DO . . .

*. . . when you're impatient
with others?*

ARE PEOPLE GETTING ON YOUR NERVES?
Are you finding it hard to get along
with others in your home, your work-
place? Try forgiveness. What if they
keep bothering you? Keep forgiving.

*Then Peter came and said to him, "Lord, . . . how
often should I forgive? As many as seven times?"*

*Jesus said to him, "Not seven times, but, I tell
you, seventy-seven times."*

—Matthew 18:21-22

YOU CAN'T BLAME PETER FOR TRYING
to put a limit on forgiveness: Wasn't

seven times enough? Peter probably thought he was being very magnanimous. But Peter was forgetting how often he needed forgiveness. Look through the gospel stories and you'll find more than seven times when Peter said or did the wrong thing. And with his bravado, when he did something wrong, he did it in a big way.

Fortunately for Peter, and for us, Jesus' idea of forgiveness was boundless. Not seven, but 77. In Jewish thought during Peter's time, seven was the number of completion, of perfection. Peter was trying to find completion in a reasonable number of offenses, but Jesus trumped him. Take your perfect number and perfect that. Keep forgiving, and forgiving, and forgiving.

. . . when others criticize you?

If the world hates you, be aware that it hated me before it hated you.

—John 15:18

$\mathscr{T}$HE YOUNG ACTRESS HAD TWO directors for the high school musical. Mr. P, the stage director, was always supportive, encouraging. "You're doing great. Now try it with a bit more energy." But the musical director, Mrs. S, was harsh and demanding. "You have no energy! You are boring the audience to death!"

Of course, the girl loved the gentle stage director and hated the critical musical director. But it was the scathing

criticism that got results. She greatly improved her performance every time Mrs. S yelled at her.

The stage director was well aware of this "good cop, bad cop" routine. Once, when the girl was complaining about Mrs. S, he stopped her. "I make you feel

better," he explained, "but she makes you better."

That's the way it often goes with criticism. We hate it. We want to think we're doing just fine. And we do need supporters to encourage us. But criticism gives us valuable information—even when it is meant to hurt us. Of course, you can't believe everything your critics say, but sift through it. Maybe there's a point of constructive criticism in there.

Blessed are you when people revile you and persecute you and utter all kinds of evil against you falsely on my account. Rejoice and be glad, for your reward is great in heaven, for in the same way they persecuted the prophets who were before you.

—Matthew 5:11-12

WHAT WOULD JESUS DO . . .

*. . . when you're holding
a grudge?*

✧

PSYCHOLOGISTS TELL US THAT grudges hurt us. Hurt held within can poison our attitudes, our relationships, our lives. But Jesus' message sets us free. We can let the hurt go because we are forgiven. Forgiven people need to forgive others. If you are aware of how much God has forgiven you, then it really doesn't matter how badly someone else has hurt you. You must forgive.

Lord, let me let it go.
I've been clinging to the stinging
Stabbing of my heart,
Holding tight to my hatred
Of the one who caused my hurt.
But now I'm growing weary,
Fearing that this hateful feeling
Will never let me grow.
So I'm finally seeking healing.
Lord, let me let it go.

WHAT WOULD JESUS DO . . .

. . . when you need courage?

And early in the morning he [Jesus] came walking toward them on the sea. But when the disciples saw him walking on the sea, they were terrified, saying, "It is a ghost!" And they cried out in fear.

But immediately Jesus spoke to them and said, "Take heart, it is I; do not be afraid."

Peter answered him, "Lord, if it is you, command me to come to you on the water."

He said, "Come."

So Peter got out of the boat, started walking on the water, and came toward Jesus. But when he noticed the strong wind, he became frightened, and beginning to sink, he cried out, "Lord, save me!"

Jesus immediately reached out his hand and caught him, saying to him, "You of little faith, why did you doubt?" When they got into the boat, the wind ceased.

—Matthew 14:25-32

PETER GETS A LOT OF BAD PRESS FOR thinking and sinking. But we should admire him for stepping out of the boat to begin with. You don't see James and John trying to waterski without skis.

Only impetuous Peter has the nerve
to join Jesus on the rolling waves.

Where does Peter get that kind
of courage? From Jesus, of course.
When the disciples first saw the figure
approaching them on the sea, they
figured it was a ghost. And that would
mean a watery grave for them. But Jesus
says, "Take heart, it is I; do not be
afraid."

Jesus says the same thing to us as
we're tossed by the waves of life. We
may be frightened by the situations we
encounter. We may worry that we're
doomed for sure. But Jesus calls to us,
"Do not be afraid. I am here with you.
Take heart!"

Buoyed by his bolstering, we can do
something as nutty as stepping out of

the boat—nowadays they call it our "comfort zone"—and walking on uncertain footing to join Jesus. As long as we keep our eyes on him, he gives us the courage to keep walking.

I hereby command you: Be strong and courageous; do not be frightened or dismayed, for the Lord your God is with you wherever you go.
—Joshua 1:9

∽

THOUGH HE SPENT MANY YEARS
leading his people there, Moses never
entered the Promised Land. God
wouldn't let him.

Hannah prayed to have a child, and
her prayers were answered, but she
never got to raise her son.

David never built the Temple,
though he selected the site and made
the plans. God reserved that privilege
for his son, Solomon.

Jeremiah faithfully proclaimed God's
message, but no one wanted to hear it.

He was regularly abused, verbally and physically.

John the Baptist paved the way for Jesus, but he was thrown in jail and never got to see most of Jesus' miracles.

Mary was "blessed among women" for giving birth to Jesus. In his adulthood, however, he spent very little time with her.

James and John, after traipsing around with Jesus for a few years, asked for positions of power in his new gov-

ernment, but he offered them only suffering.

Paul prayed for the removal of his "thorn in the flesh"—some mysterious ailment—but was told he'd have to live with it.

Life can be very disappointing, even if you're a giant of the faith. Live a certain way and you expect certain rewards. When things don't turn out as you hope, you feel cheated. You say with the Psalmist: "All in vain I have kept my heart clean and washed my hands in innocence. For all day long I have been plagued, and am punished every morning" (Psalm 73:13-14).

Friends disappoint us. Coworkers, bosses, family members, the government—we get disappointment from many sources, but often we trace our disappointment back to God. If he were really running the world properly, we think, he'd make things turn out better for us.

Maybe. But try to get the bigger picture. We pray, "Thy kingdom come," and God is always answering that prayer, preparing us for a future kingdom that won't disappoint us.

WHAT WOULD JESUS DO . . .

. . . when disaster strikes?

*We . . . boast in our sufferings, knowing that
suffering produces endurance, and endurance
produces character, and character produces hope,
and hope does not disappoint us, because God's
love has been poured into our hearts through the
Holy Spirit that has been given to us.*

—*Romans 5:3-5*

$\mathcal{I}$N THE 1870S, A MAN NAMED HORATIO
G. Spafford was planning a trans-Atlantic
vacation for his family. He sent his wife
and four daughters on a ship bound for
England while he finished up some
business back home in Chicago. But
tragedy struck that ship. It collided with
another vessel, killing 226 passengers—

including all of the Spafford children. Horatio boarded the next ship for England, to join his grieving wife. On the way, he wrote a hymn that has comforted millions of Christians in their times of sorrow: "It Is Well With My Soul."

When peace, like a river, attends my way,
when sorrows like sea billows roll;
whatever my lot, you have taught me to say,
"It is well, it is well with my soul."
It is well with my soul, it is well,
it is well with my soul.
And, Lord, haste the day when my faith shall be
  sight,
the clouds be rolled back as a scroll,
the trump shall sound and the Lord shall de-
  scend,
even so—it is well with my soul.

—Horatio G. Spafford

My brothers and sisters, whenever you face trials of any kind, consider it nothing but joy, because you know that the testing of your faith produces endurance; and let endurance have its full effect, so that you may be mature and complete, lacking in nothing.

—James 1:2-4

. . . *when you need more faith?*

∽

[*The father of a demon-possessed boy asked Jesus,*] " . . . *if you are able to do anything, have pity on us and help us.*"

Jesus said to him, "If you are able!—All things can be done for the one who believes."

Immediately the father of the child cried out, "I believe; help my unbelief!"

—Mark 9:22-24

$\mathcal{T}$HE BELIEVER IS ALWAYS A DOUBTER, too. Jesus encouraged faith, but he always took time for skeptical questions. He was energized by the honest struggle of belief and doubt: in

Nathanael, who was sure that Nazareth couldn't produce a prophet; in Nicodemus, who wondered how a grown man could be reborn; in the rich, young ruler, whose commitment was choked by his wealth; in some of the lawyers who grilled him; and in the father of the demon-possessed boy.

"I believe; help my unbelief!" That could be the cry of many of us, as we wrestle with eternal questions in our material world.

Now faith is the assurance of things hoped for, the conviction of things not seen.

—Hebrews 11:1

WHAT JESUS HATED WAS DISBELIEF—that is, a refusal to believe even in the face of strong evidence. He encountered many who simply did not want to trust him. They set their hearts against him, and he strongly criticized that attitude.

But if you're truly examining issues of faith, relax. Jesus will help you along in your journey of faith. He'll take whatever germ of authentic faith you have and leverage that into a powerful force.

Truly I tell you, if you have faith the size of a mustard seed, you will say to this mountain, "Move from here to there," and it will move; and nothing will be impossible for you.

—Matthew 17:20

WHAT WOULD JESUS DO . . .

. . . when you really don't love your neighbor?

"Teacher, which commandment in the law is the greatest?" He said to him, "'You shall love the Lord your God with all your heart, and with all your soul, and with all your mind.' This is the greatest and first commandment. And a second is like it: 'You shall love your neighbor as yourself.' . . . "

—Matthew 22:36-37

LATER, A LAWYER TRIED TO PIN JESUS down, asking, "Who is my neighbor?" Let's get some sort of technical definition here. Your next-door neighbor? Everyone who lives within a hundred cubits? Everyone of your own race?

In response, Jesus told the story of the Good Samaritan. A Jewish traveler gets mugged, two good Jews pass him by, and finally it's a member of the hated race of Samaritans who stops to help him. "Which of these three, do you think, was a neighbor to the man who fell into the hands of robbers?" Jesus asked. The lawyer had his answer: "The one who had mercy on him." Love of neighbor is never a matter of racial affinity, but of merciful action.

"Love your neighbor" was a well-known command from the Book of Deuteronomy, but some people had tacked on what seemed to them a logical extension: "and hate your enemy." Jesus turned that around, urging his followers to "love your enemies."

If you love those who love you, what reward do you have? Do not even the tax collectors do the same? And if you greet only your brothers and sisters, what more are you doing than others? Do not even the Gentiles do the same?

—*Matthew 5:46-47*

*S*O ARE YOU HAVING TROUBLE LOVING those around you? Join the club. Sometimes it's tough to love. People can be annoying. But try to look at them in a new light, the light of Jesus' love for them. He gave his life even for those who crucified him.

Whoever says, "I am in the light," while hating a brother or sister, is still in the darkness. Whoever loves a brother or sister lives in the light, and in such a person there is no cause for stumbling.

—*1 John 2:9-10*

. . . when you're having a hard time overcoming your past?

∞

Come now, let us argue it out, says the Lord:
though your sins are like scarlet, they shall be
like snow; though they are red like crimson, they
shall become like wool.

—Isaiah 1:18

*J*ESUS SHOCKED HIS HEARERS BY
announcing that prostitutes and corrupt
tax collectors would enter God's kingdom
ahead of the religious leaders. God's favor
didn't depend on past accomplishments.
As in many modern hiring situations, it's
not what you've done, it's who you know.

. . . the righteousness of God through faith in Jesus Christ [is] for all who believe. For there is no distinction, since all have sinned and fall short of the glory of God; they are now justified by his grace as a gift, through the redemption that is in Christ Jesus.

—Romans 3:22-24

I was formerly a blasphemer, a persecutor, and a man of violence. But I received mercy because I had acted ignorantly in unbelief, and the grace of our Lord overflowed for me with the faith and love that are in Christ Jesus. The saying is sure and worthy of full acceptance, that Christ Jesus came into the world to save sinners—of whom I am the foremost.

—The Apostle Paul
(1 Timothy 1:13-15)

*P*AUL WAS THE POSTER CHILD FOR forgiveness. If anyone had forfeited his favor with God, it was this persecutor

of Christians. But Jesus met him and changed his life.

Look around the Bible and the pattern repeats. God has shown his love for many sinners: Jacob the trickster, Rahab the prostitute, David the adulterer. So quit clinging to the shame of your past and let God love you!

The Lord is merciful and gracious, slow to anger and abounding in steadfast love. He will not always accuse, nor will he keep his anger forever. He does not deal with us according to our sins, nor repay us according to our iniqui-

ties. For as the heavens are high above the earth, so great is his steadfast love toward those who fear him; as far as the east is from the west, so far he removes our transgressions from us. As a father has compassion for his children, so the Lord has compassion for those who fear him. For he knows how we were made; he remembers that we are dust.

—Psalm 103:8-14

WHAT WOULD JESUS DO . . .

. . . when you feel like giving up?

Have you not known? Have you not heard?
The Lord is the everlasting God, the Creator of
the ends of the earth. He does not faint or grow
weary; his understanding is unsearchable. He
gives power to the faint, and strengthens the
powerless. Even youths will faint and be weary,
and the young will fall exhausted; but those
who wait for the Lord shall renew their strength,
they shall mount up with wings like eagles, they
shall run and not be weary, they shall walk and
not faint.

—Isaiah 40:28-31

I'm tired, Lord.

Beaten down, defeated.

I feel like I've run a marathon but there are still miles to go.

I've swum halfway across the ocean and I can't continue—

Now I just have to swim back.

I've tried, I really have.

I want to do right.

I want to conquer sin.

I want to make a positive difference in the world, in my world.

But I keep goofing up.

Not just minor malfunctions, but major disasters.

I really know how to make a mess of things.

I'm tired, Lord.

I want to give up.

Can you help me out . . . again?

But thanks be to God, who gives us the victory through our Lord Jesus Christ. Therefore, my beloved, be steadfast, immovable, always excelling in the work of the Lord, because you know that in the Lord your labor is not in vain.

—1 Corinthians 15:57-58

WHAT WOULD JESUS DO ...

... when it seems that God doesn't care?

A great windstorm arose, and the waves beat into the boat, so that the boat was already being swamped. But he was in the stern, asleep on the cushion; and they woke him up and said to him, "Teacher, do you not care that we are perishing?"

He woke up and rebuked the wind, and said to the sea, "Peace! Be still!" Then the wind ceased, and there was a dead calm. He said to them, "Why are you afraid? Have you still no faith?"

And they were filled with great awe and said to one another, "Who then is this, that even the wind and the sea obey him?"

—Mark 4:37-40

*I*N THE STORM-TOSSED BOAT, THE disciples had plenty of reasons for alarm. A number of them were fishermen, and they'd probably weathered a few storms before, so this must have been a doozy. Yet Jesus slept through it—until they woke him up, screaming, "Don't you care?"

We do the same thing in the storms of our lives, don't we? We're sending out an SOS while the Lord seems to be grabbing some Zs. "Don't you care if we drown in our troubles, Lord?"

Yes, he cares. As Jesus roused himself from his nap, he questioned the faith of his friends. Their fear had chased away their faith. They doubted that he had the power to tame the tempest, and even if he did, they weren't sure whether he cared enough to help them. Those are the two prongs of our anxiety, too. Sometimes our terrors seem too big for even God. We can't imagine any way out. And why would he stoop to help little old us, anyway? Why should he care?

Are not five sparrows sold for two pennies? Yet not one of them is forgotten in God's sight. But even the hairs of your head are all counted. Do not be afraid; you are of more value than many sparrows.

—Luke 12:6-7

$\mathcal{G}$OD IS INFINITELY POWERFUL. HE'S also infinitely caring. He can reach the farthest galaxy, but also the tiniest quark. He loves sparrows a lot, and he loves us even more.

. . . when you're afraid?

Do not fear, for I am with you, do not be afraid, for I am your God; I will strengthen you, I will help you, I will uphold you with my victorious right hand.

—Isaiah 41:10

ONE OF THE MOST COMMON PHRASES in the gospels is "don't be afraid," appearing more than 20 times. Often, it's Jesus reassuring the people around him. Amid storms of nature and threats of persecution, the followers of Jesus could stand secure.

Peace I leave with you; my peace I give to you. I do not give to you as the world gives. Do not

*let your hearts be troubled, and do not let them
be afraid.*

—John 14:27

*T*HE "PEACE" THAT THE WORLD GIVES
is often escape, distraction. In the
movies, troubled people are always
reaching for a drink. Psychologists tell
us our first reaction to terror is denial:
"This is not happening."

But Christ offers a peace with eyes
wide open. Whatever the threat, you
are held in the Lord's hands. You can
stare down pain and loss because you
know you have a powerful comforter.
Let the frightful circumstances lead you
to a greater dependence on God. Fear
the Lord, and there's nothing else to
fear.

How sweet the name of Jesus sounds
In a believer's ear!
It soothes his sorrows, heals his wounds,
And drives away his fear.

—John Newton

We don't know what the future holds, but we
*   know who holds the future.*

—Traditional saying

WHAT WOULD JESUS DO . . .

. . . when children are driving you crazy?

☙

Then little children were being brought to him in order that he might lay his hands on them and pray. The disciples spoke sternly to those who brought them; but Jesus said, "Let the little children come to me, and do not stop them; for it is to such as these that the kingdom of heaven belongs." And he laid his hands on them and went on his way.

—Matthew 19:13-15

CHILDREN ARE SMALL, LOUD, AND messy. Sure, they can be cute, but that effect tends to wear off after a few minutes of whining, sniveling, or crying. They're distracting, too. They keep grown-ups from conducting important grown-up business.

All of this was almost certainly running through the disciples' minds as they "protected" Jesus from these tiny creatures. We're not sure what they said when they "spoke sternly" to the parents, but it was probably along the lines of "don't waste the Savior's time. Jesus has more important things to do than wipe noses."

That sounds harsh to us in our Mister Rogers era, but the ancient world had little time for youngsters. The disciples were just reflecting a common prejudice: Children weren't worth much, at least until they could help with chores.

But then it was Jesus' turn to speak sternly. Children? Why, that's what it's all about. The disciples had obviously forgotten his lesson from the previous chapter. Jesus had brought a little child before them and said, "Unless you change and become like children, you will never enter the kingdom of heaven" (Matthew 18:2-3).

What did he mean by all that? Children are learners, curious enough to

stick their little fingers into anything. They're open to new ideas, because everything is new to them. Children don't know much yet, and they can't do much yet, but they generally recognize that they need loving parents to help them out.

If grown-ups were more like kids, Jesus was saying, they would know how much help they need from their loving Heavenly Parent. You don't barge into God's kingdom with your ten-page résumé in hand. You enter humbly, as a child.

And that's something to remember as your kids are running you ragged. They need so much guidance, so much discipline, so much love. Don't we all? Seriously, Jesus treasured children because they were so needy—and so honest about their need. So, even as they're taxing your patience, eating paste and scribbling on wallpaper, they're teaching you something important about your relationship with God.

. . . when you're lonely?

And going a little farther, he threw himself on the ground and prayed, "My Father, if it is possible, let this cup pass from me; yet not what I want but what you want." Then he came to the disciples and found them sleeping; and he said to Peter, "So, could you not stay awake with me one hour?"

—Matthew 26:39-40

WE GET A GLIMPSE OF JESUS' LONE-liness in the Garden of Gethsemane. The gospels often show him surrounded by crowds of people, traveling with 12 disciples and other friends, but there must have been times when he felt that no one understood him. In the garden, he knew trouble was coming. He was about to be arrested, and within 24 hours crucified and buried. This was the "cup" of suffering the Father was offering him and, to be honest, he didn't want to drink it.

In his time of anguish, he took his three closest friends with him to pray, but they fell asleep. Obviously, they didn't understand how impor-  tant this moment was. The salvation of the world depended on Jesus' decision to go through with the Father's plan, and he could have used a little support.

In prayer, however, Jesus renewed his commitment to his Father and he went on with the task assigned to him.

You might try the same approach when you're lonely. Instead of running out to find new friends, use the time to talk with God. Listen for his voice in the "sheer silence" of the moment and commit yourself to do what he wants. Then follow through on that commitment, carrying out the task God gives you.

WHAT WOULD JESUS DO...

...when someone makes you angry?

∽

When they came to the place that is called The Skull, they crucified Jesus there with the criminals, one on his right and one on his left. Then Jesus said, "Father, forgive them; for they do not know what they are doing."

—Luke 23:33-34

*I*T'S NATURAL FOR YOU TO GET steamed when you see something wrong going on, especially when you're the victim. What can you do about it?

First, *get the big picture.* Maybe you're misunderstanding the situation. Say you're walking down a crowded street and someone bumps into you, hard!

You whirl around to yell at the incon-
siderate oaf—but then you see it's a
disabled person struggling along on
crutches. Your anger melts because you
see the situation differently.

By all rights, Jesus should have been
angry as he hung on the cross. He was
completely innocent, and yet he was
suffering a cruel execution. But he
understood that they were acting from
ignorance, and that softened his reaction. We can often find forgiveness in
our hearts for others as we recognize
their limitations.

*. . . Jesus went up to Jerusalem. In the temple he
found people selling cattle, sheep, and doves, and
the money changers seated at their tables. Making a whip of cords, he drove all of them out of
the temple, both the sheep and the cattle. He also*

poured out the coins of the money changers and overturned their tables. He told those who were selling the doves, "Take these things out of here! Stop making my Father's house a marketplace!" His disciples remembered that it was written, "Zeal for your house will consume me."

—John 2:13-17

*J*ESUS GOT ANGRY! THAT'S A LIBERATING notion for all those who have learned to stuff their rage in the name of religion. If someone makes you angry, you don't need to deny your feelings—but you should be careful about them.

Sometimes you can soften your

feelings by "getting the big picture," but other times you face real injustice, as Jesus did with the money changers in the Temple. Then you can try to *correct the situation.* Don't just vent your feelings; make a positive change. Sometimes a strong statement can do the trick; other times action is required.

Be angry but do not sin; do not let the sun go down on your anger.

—Ephesians 4:26

$\mathcal{U}$LTIMATELY IT'S IMPORTANT TO DEAL wisely with your anger. Don't stuff it; let it out! But control yourself enough to avoid sinful actions, such as the spiteful hurting of others. You don't want to escalate a battle, but you do want to get rid of your rage. Don't let it simmer overnight. Then it's sure to boil over later, and it'll do you some damage in the meantime.